60 Great Cowboy Movie Posters

volume twenty-one of
the illustrated history of movies through posters

Images from the Hershenson-Allen Archive

Previous Volumes:

Volume One: Cartoon Movie Posters
Volume Two: Cowboy Movie Posters
Volume Three: Academy Award® Winners' Movie Posters
Volume Four: Sports Movie Posters
Volume Five: Crime Movie Posters
Volume Six: More Cowboy Movie Posters
Volume Seven: Horror Movie Posters
Volume Eight: Best Pictures' Movie Posters
Volume Nine: Musical Movie Posters
Volume Ten: Serial Movie Posters
Volume Eleven: Horror, Sci-Fi & Fantasy Movie Posters
Volume Twelve: Comedy Movie Posters
Volume Thirteen: War Movie Posters
Volume Fourteen: Attack of the "B" Movie Posters
Volume Fifteen: Not Nominated. Movie Posters
Volume Sixteen: To Be Continued… Movie Posters
Volume Seventeen: Who Goes There? Movie Posters
Volume Eighteen: Drive-In Movie Posters
Volume Nineteen: 60 Great Horror Movie Posters
Volume Twenty: 60 Great Sci-Fi Movie Posters

Published by Bruce Hershenson
P.O. Box 874, West Plains, MO 65775
Phone: (417) 256-9616 Fax: (417) 257-6948
mail@brucehershenson.com (e-mail)
http://www.brucehershenson.com or
http://www.emovieposter.com (website)

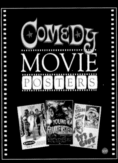

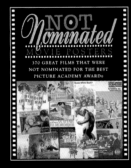

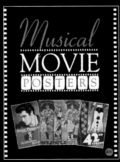

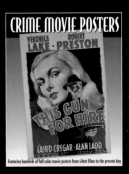

INTRODUCTION

Welcome to a new series of full-color movie poster books from Bruce Hershenson Publishing! Over the past nine years I have published eighteen volumes of a series of full-color books called the Illustrated History of Movies Through Posters. Each of those volumes is devoted to a specific genre or category of film (horror, cowboy, crime, Academy Award Winners, etc) and each contains hundreds of full-color images from that genre, each containing the finest color printing there is, equal or superior to that found in coffee table books costing several times the price!

While these books have been extremely well received by collectors and movie buffs world-wide, the one request I have regularly received since I began publishing has been to include more full-page images in each volume (in order to give a wide-ranging overview of each topic, I needed to print five images on most pages, although each volume has some full-page images). But I certainly understand a small image does not do justice to these great posters, and I have always agonized when deciding which posters will be given a full page!

That is why I have made this major change to the series. Each new volume in this series now contains sixty of the finest posters from a single genre, with EVERY poster receiving a full-page and each volume is printed with the exact same standards of quality of the earlier series. Since the cover price of each volume is just $14.99, that means the cost per image is just 25 cents!

For this volume, 60 Great Cowboy Movie Posters, I was faced with an unusual problem. Three of the greatest cowboy stars, John Wayne, Buck Jones, and Tom Mix, were great moneymakers for their studios and those studios (Republic, Columbia, and William Fox) created their finest posters for their films. So this book could have consisted entirely of posters of those three stars! But I wanted to still give an overview of all the top stars over all the years, so I chose some of the finest posters of the above stars and also many of the finest posters of the other top cowboy stars, and the best-remembered western films.

Where did the images in this book come from? They are contained within the archive I co-own with my partner, Richard Allen, the Hershenson-Allen Archive. The archive consists of over 35,000 different movie poster images, all photographed directly from the original posters onto high quality 4" x 5" color transparencies. There is not another resource like it anywhere, and it is the world,s foremost source of movie poster images. The Archive has provided images for books, videos, DVDs, magazines, and newspapers.

All of the images in this volume are of the original U.S. one-sheet poster (the standard movie poster size, measuring 27" x 41"), from the first release of the film. There are certainly many other size cowboy posters (and posters from other countries) that are superlative, and I hope to include those in a future volume of this series.

This is not a catalog of posters for sale, nor do I sell any sort of movie poster reproductions! However, I do sell movie posters of all sorts through auctions, primarily over the Internet, and in the past 14 years I have sold over 17 million dollars of movie paper! If you are interested in acquiring original vintage movie posters (or any of the other 34 books I have published) visit my website at **http://www.brucehershenson.com** (the most visited vintage movie poster site on the Internet with over 500,000 visitors to date) or send a self-addressed stamped envelope to the address on the title page for free brochures.

I need to thank Amy Knight who did the layouts and designed the covers for this book, and Courier Graphics, who printed it. Most of all, I need to thank my partner, Richard Allen. He has always loved movie posters of all years and genres, and he helped track down the images in this book. We share a common vision, and we hope to keep publishing these volumes until we have covered every possible genre of film.

I dedicate this book to my mother, Gloria Weiner. She has been a constant source of support to me throughout my life, and I can't thank her enough!

Bruce Hershenson
June 2003

GLOSSARY

1 . . . . THE COLD DECK, 1917
2 . . . . A DEBTOR TO THE LAW, 1919
3 . . . . LIGHTNING BRYCE, 1919
4 . . . . WEST IS WEST, 1920
5 . . . . THE BULL-DOGGER, 1921
6 . . . . THE FOX, 1921
7 . . . . THE HALF BREED, 1922
8 . . . . THE COVERED WAGON, 1923
9 . . . . DON Q SON OF ZORRO, 1925
10 . . . . TUMBLEWEEDS, 1925
11 . . . . THE VANISHING AMERICAN, 1925
12 . . . . THE GREAT K&A TRAIN ROBBERY, 1926
13 . . . . THE LAST OUTLAW, 1927
14 . . . . KING COWBOY, 1928
15 . . . . UNDER THE TONTO RIM, 1928
16 . . . . THE WAGON SHOW, 1928
17 . . . . GUN LAW, 1929
18 . . . . SPOILERS, 1930
19 . . . . CIMARRON, 1931
20 . . . . DESERT VENGEANCE, 1931
21 . . . . RIDIN' FOR JUSTICE, 1931
22 . . . . FORBIDDEN TRAIL, 1932
23 . . . . SOUTH OF THE RIO GRANDE, 1932
24 . . . . WHITE EAGLE, 1932
25 . . . . MAN OF ACTION, 1933
26 . . . . THE CHEYENNE KID, 1933
27 . . . . GORDON OF GHOST CITY, 1933
28 . . . . UNKNOWN VALLEY, 1933
29 . . . . TERROR TRAIL, 1933
30 . . . . THE PRESCOTT KID, 1934
31 . . . . WAGON WHEELS, 1934
32 . . . . PARADISE CANYON, 1935
33 . . . . THE LONELY TRAIL, 1936
34 . . . . HOPALONG CASSIDY RETURNS, 1936
35 . . . . OREGON TRAIL, 1936
36 . . . . THE SINGING COWBOY, 1936
37 . . . . THE PLAINSMAN, 1936
38 . . . . BOOTS OF DESTINY, 1937
39 . . . . GIT ALONG LITTLE DOGIES, 1937
40 . . . . BAR 20 JUSTICE, 1938
41 . . . . THE LONE RANGER, 1938
42 . . . . PRIDE OF THE WEST, 1938
43 . . . . THE TEXANS, 1938
44 . . . . DODGE CITY, 1939
45 . . . . IN OLD CALIENTE, 1939
46 . . . . STAGECOACH, 1939
47 . . . . THE OKLAHOMA KID, 1939
48 . . . . JESSE JAMES, 1939
49 . . . . BELLE STARR, 1941
50 . . . . THE OUTLAW, 1943
51 . . . . BROKEN ARROW, 1950
52 . . . . THE LONE RANGER, 1956
53 . . . . THE ALAMO, 1960
54 . . . . HIGH PLAINSDRIFTER, 1973
55 . . . . THE OUTLAW JOSEY WALES, 1976
56 . . . . THE OUTLAW JOSEY WALES, 1976
57 . . . . THE SHOOTIST, 1976
58 . . . . PALE RIDER, 1985
59 . . . . PALE RIDER, 1985
60 . . . . UNFORGIVEN, 1992

S·A·LYNCH ENTERPRISES, INC.
PRESENT
WM S·HART
in
THE COLD DECK
A SUPERLATIVE PRODUCTION

1

PAN-AMERICAN
MOTION PICTURE CORP.
PRESENTS

Henry Starr
--- IN ---
A DEBTOR TO THE LAW

THE NORMAN FILM MFG. CO.
PRESENTS

BILL PICKETT
WORLD'S COLORED CHAMPION —IN—
"THE BULL-DOGGER"
Featuring The Colored Hero of the Mexican Bull Ring in Death Defying Feats of Courage and Skill.
THRILLS! LAUGHS TOO!
Produced by NORMAN FILM MFG. CO.
JACKSONVILLE, FLA.

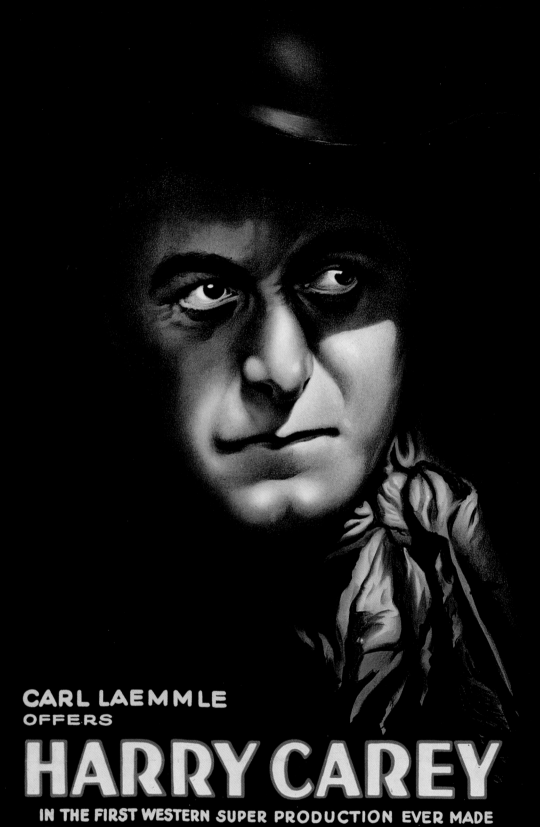

CARL LAEMMLE
OFFERS

HARRY CAREY

IN THE FIRST WESTERN SUPER PRODUCTION EVER MADE

THE FOX

DIRECTED BY ROBERT THORNBY

UNIVERSAL-JEWEL MASTERPIECE

The cowards never started:— The weak died on the way.

JESSE L. LASKY *Presents* a
JAMES CRUZE *Production*
THE COVERED WAGON

ADAPTED BY JACK CUNNINGHAM
FROM THE NOVEL BY EMERSON HOUGH

a Paramount Picture

8

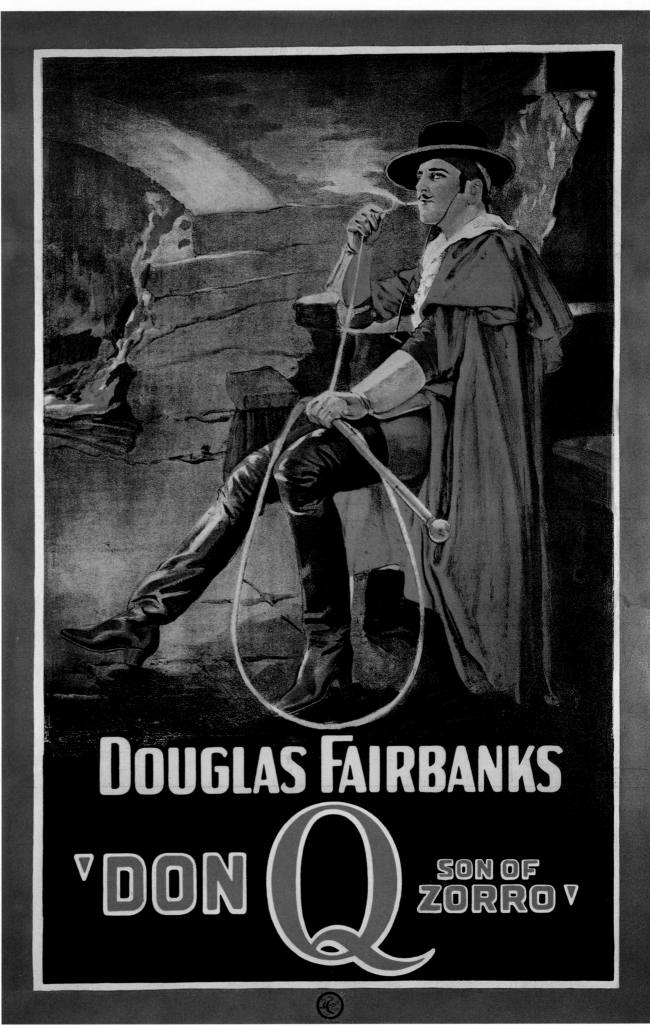

WILLIAM S. HART
IN
'TUMBLEWEEDS'

Story by *Hal G. Evarts* . *Adapted for the Screen by* **C. Gardner Sullivan**

DIRECTED BY **KING BAGGOT**

A **WILLIAM S. HART** PRODUCTION

-a *United Artists* Picture-

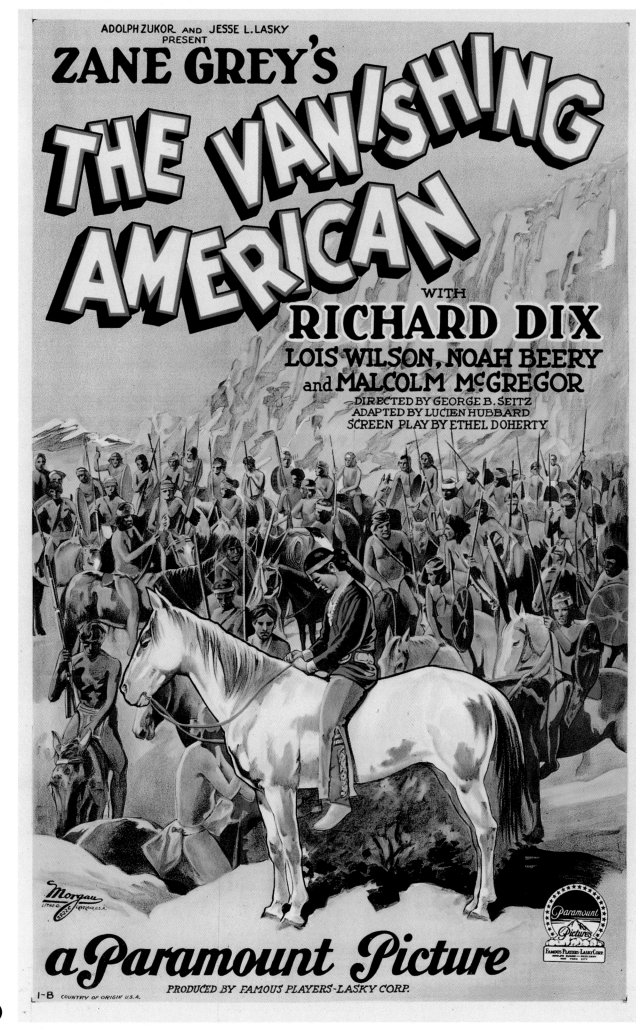

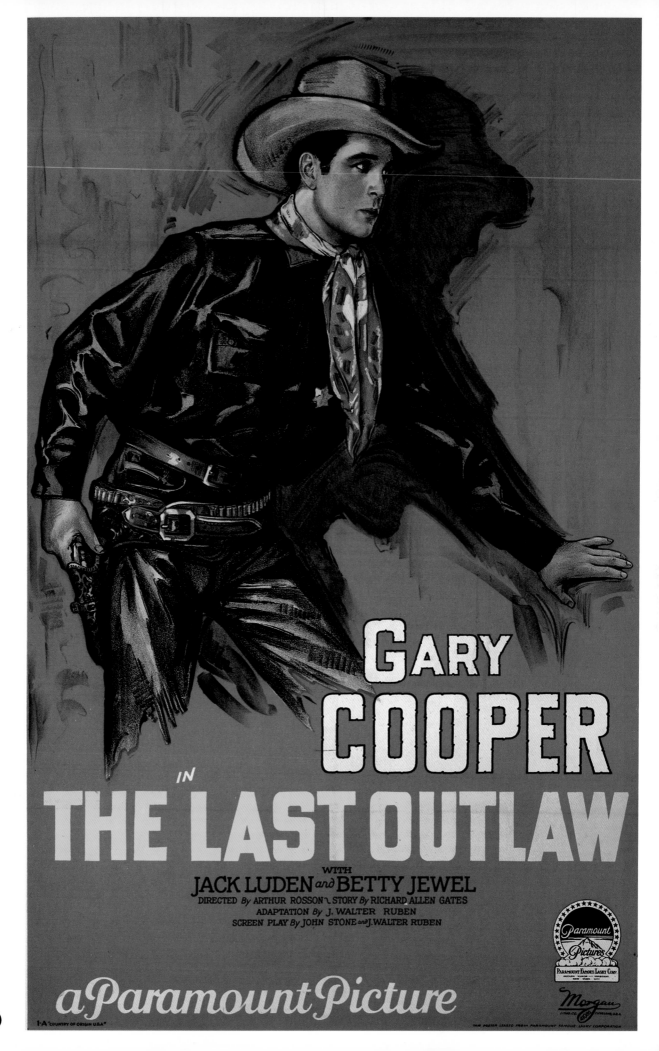

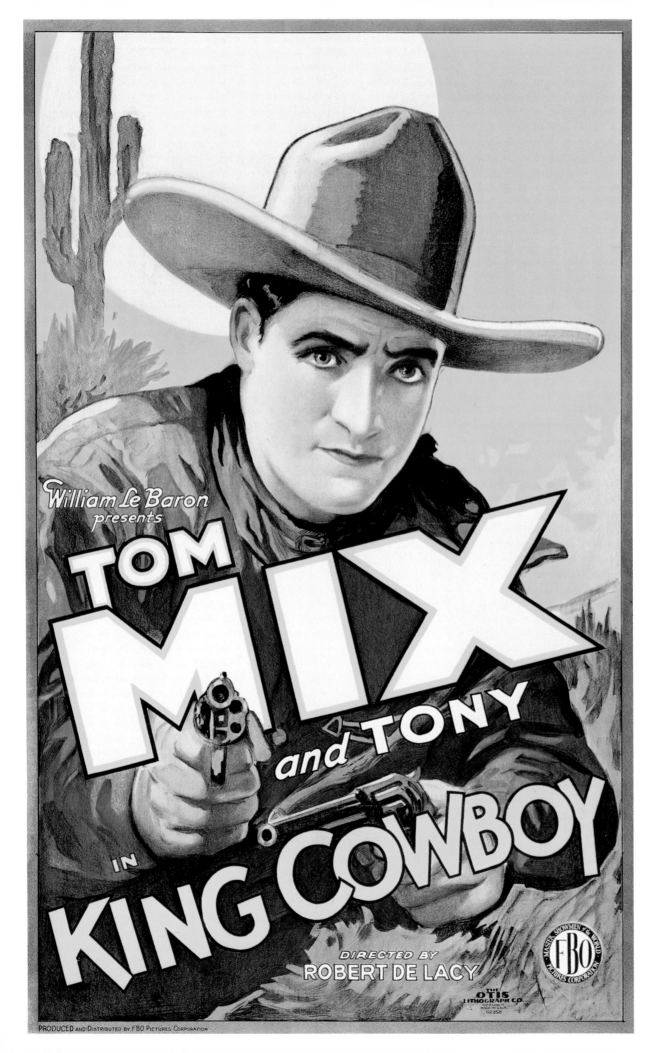

ZANE GREY'S

UNDER the TONTO RIM

WITH
RICHARD ARLEN and MARY BRIAN

DIRECTED by HERMAN C. RAYMAKER
FROM A NOVEL by ZANE GREY
SCREEN PLAY by J. WALTER RUBEN

a Paramount Picture

15

REX BEACH'S
THE SPOILERS

AN EDWIN CAREWE PRODUCTION

With
GARY COOPER
KAY JOHNSON AND BETTY COMPSON
a Paramount Picture

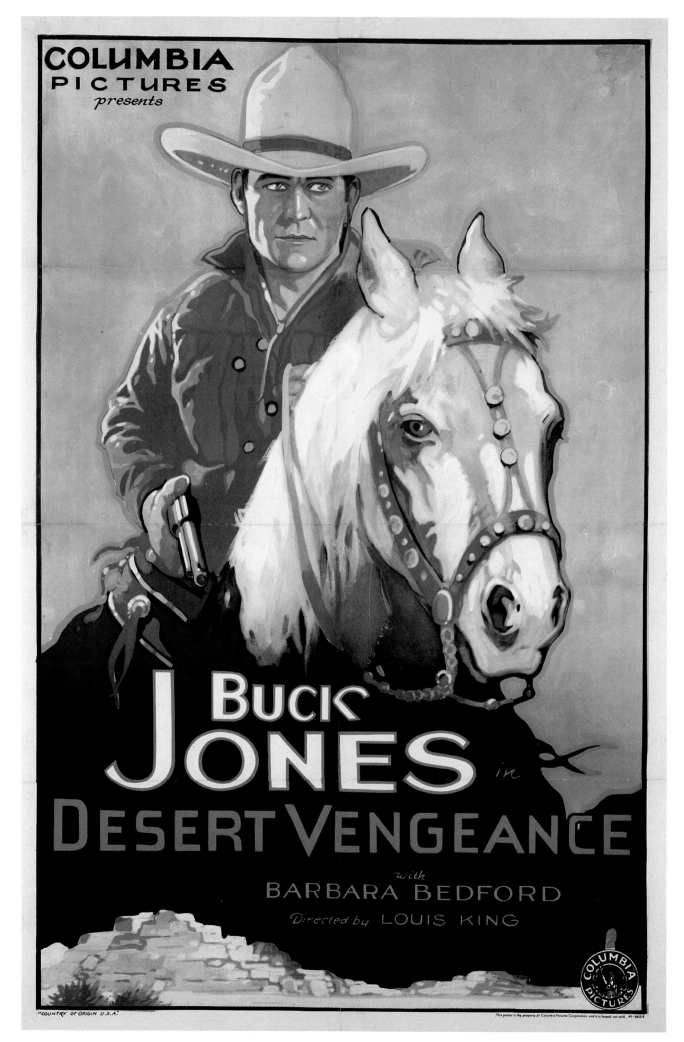

21

Riding for Life - for Honor - and for LOVE!

BUCK JONES in "FORBIDDEN TRAIL"
with BARBARA WEEKS • MARY CARR
DIRECTED BY LAMBERT HILLYER
A COLUMBIA PICTURE

COLUMBIA PICTURES

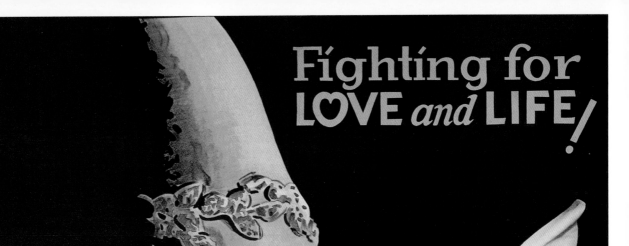

Fighting for
LOVE and LIFE!

Buck
JONES
in
"SOUTH
of the RIO
GRANDE"

with
MONA MARIS
DORIS HILL
Directed by
LAMBERT HILLYER

A COLUMBIA PICTURE

23

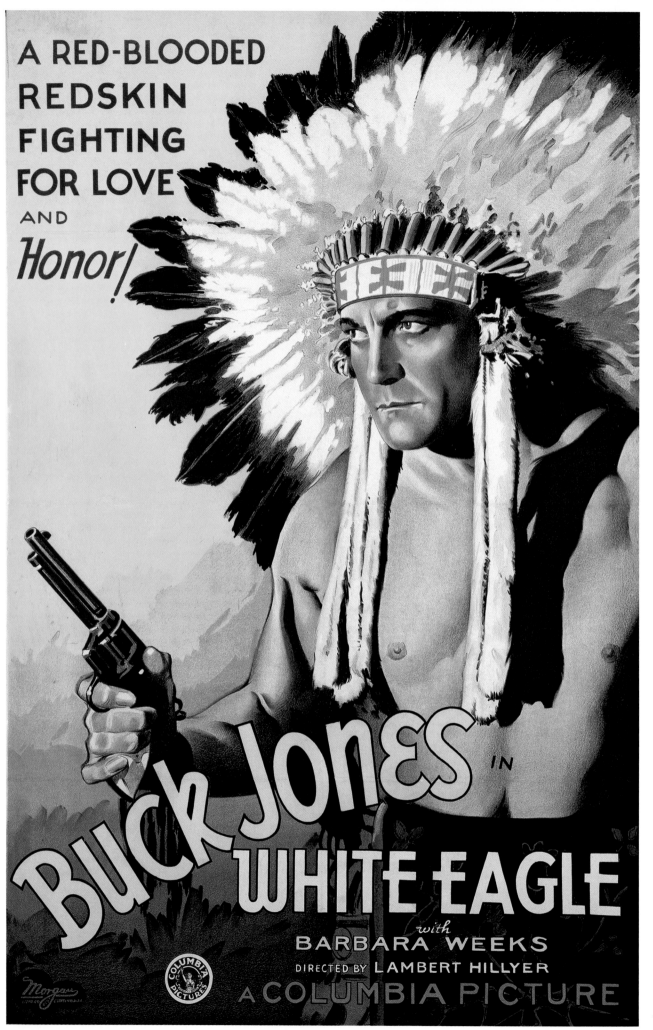

A RED-BLOODED REDSKIN FIGHTING FOR LOVE AND *Honor!*

BUCK JONES IN WHITE EAGLE

with BARBARA WEEKS

DIRECTED BY LAMBERT HILLYER

A COLUMBIA PICTURE

COLUMBIA PICTURES

24

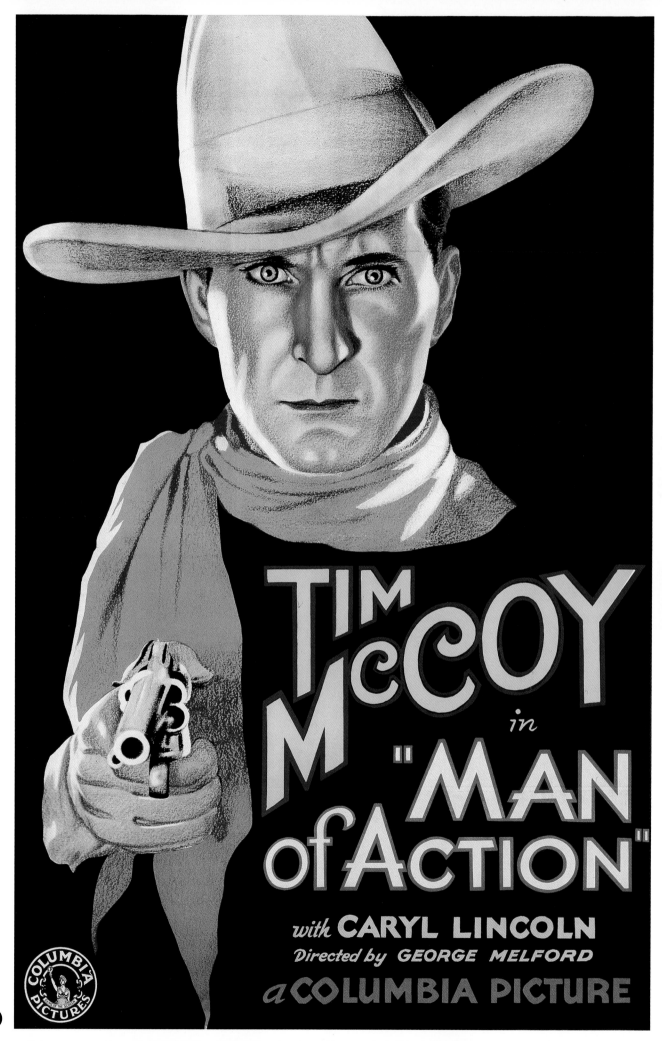

TIM McCOY in "MAN of ACTION"

with CARYL LINCOLN
Directed by GEORGE MELFORD
a COLUMBIA PICTURE

COLUMBIA PICTURES

25

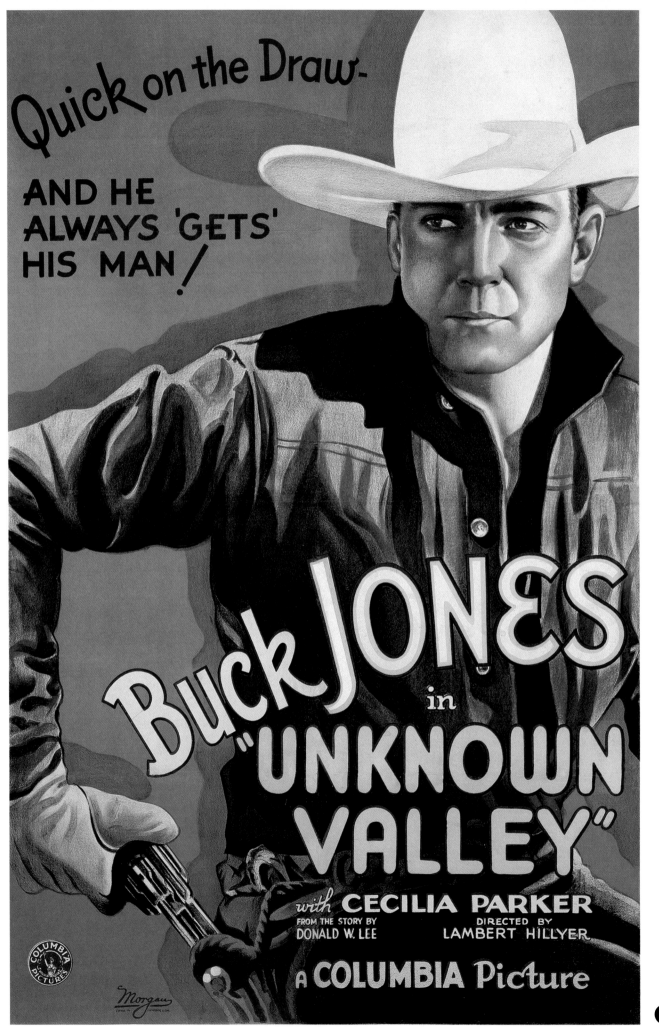

Quick on the Draw—
AND HE ALWAYS 'GETS' HIS MAN!

Buck JONES in "UNKNOWN VALLEY"
with CECILIA PARKER
FROM THE STORY BY DONALD W. LEE
DIRECTED BY LAMBERT HILLYER
A COLUMBIA Picture

BRANDED A THIEF — VINDICATED BY *Love!*

Tim McCOY
in

The Prescott Kid
with
SHEILA MANNORS
FROM THE STORY BY CLAUDE RISTER
Directed by DAVID SELMAN

A COLUMBIA PICTURE ..

COLUMBIA PICTURES

ADOLPH ZUKOR presents

ZANE GREY'S

WAGON wheels

WITH RANDOLPH SCOTT, GAIL PATRICK
MONTE BLUE, RAYMOND HATTON
BILLY LEE
A PARAMOUNT PICTURE

31

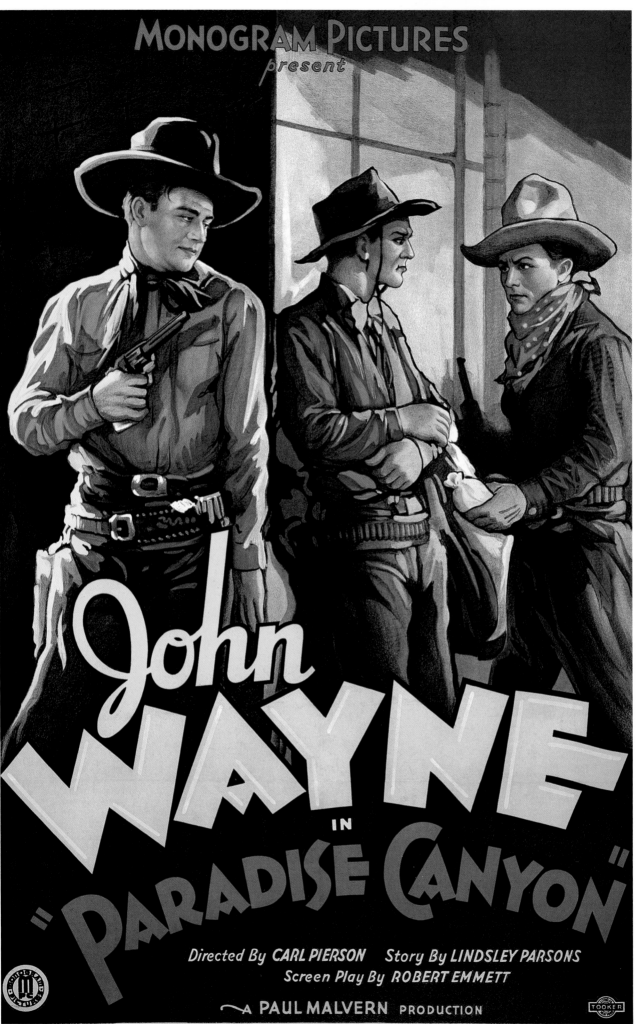

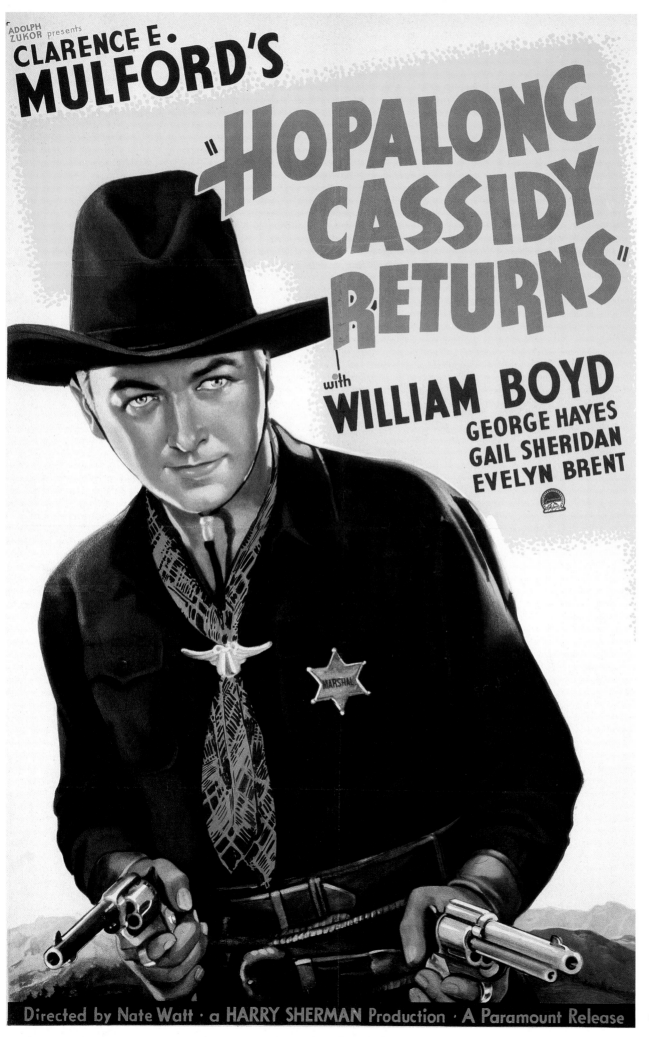

REPUBLIC PICTURES *presents*

GENE AUTRY IN

"The SINGING COWBOY"

with
SMILEY BURNETTE
and "CHAMPION"

DIRECTED BY MACK WRIGHT
SUPERVISED BY ARMAND SCHAEFER
SCREENPLAY BY DORRELL and STUART McGOWAN
ORIGINAL STORY BY TOM GIBSON
Produced by NAT LEVINE

REPUBLIC PICTURES

A REPUBLIC PICTURE

ADOLPH ZUKOR presents

GARY COOPER   JEAN ARTHUR

IN

CECIL B. DeMILLE'S

"THE PLAINSMAN"

WITH
JAMES ELLISON · CHARLES BICKFORD   Directed by CECIL B. DeMILLE
A PARAMOUNT PICTURE

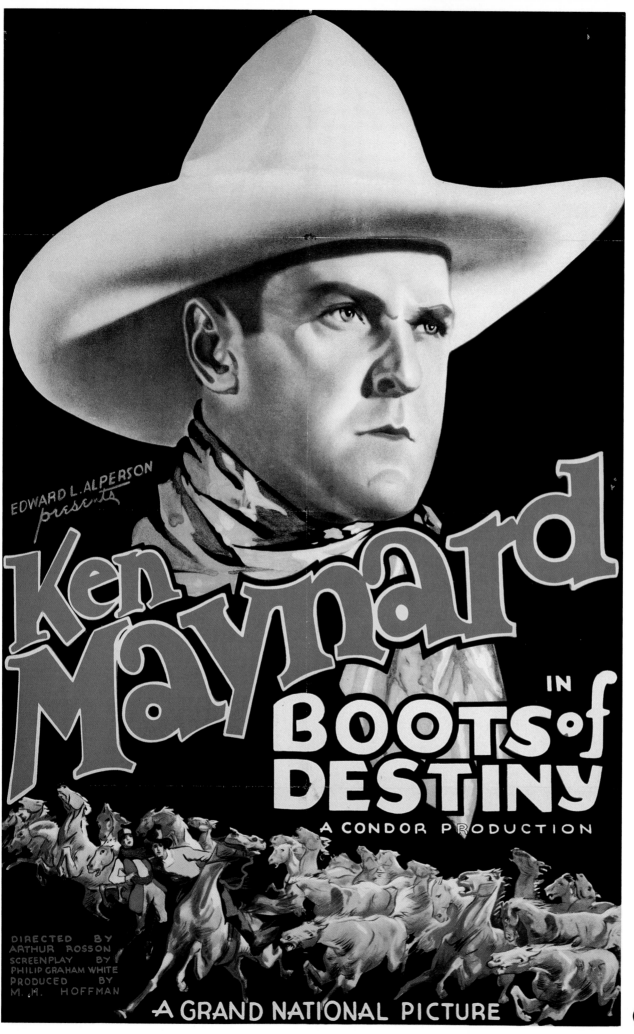

EDWARD L. ALPERSON
presents

Ken Maynard

IN

BOOTS of DESTINY

A CONDOR PRODUCTION

DIRECTED BY
ARTHUR ROSSON
SCREENPLAY BY
PHILIP GRAHAM WHITE
PRODUCED BY
M. H. HOFFMAN

A GRAND NATIONAL PICTURE

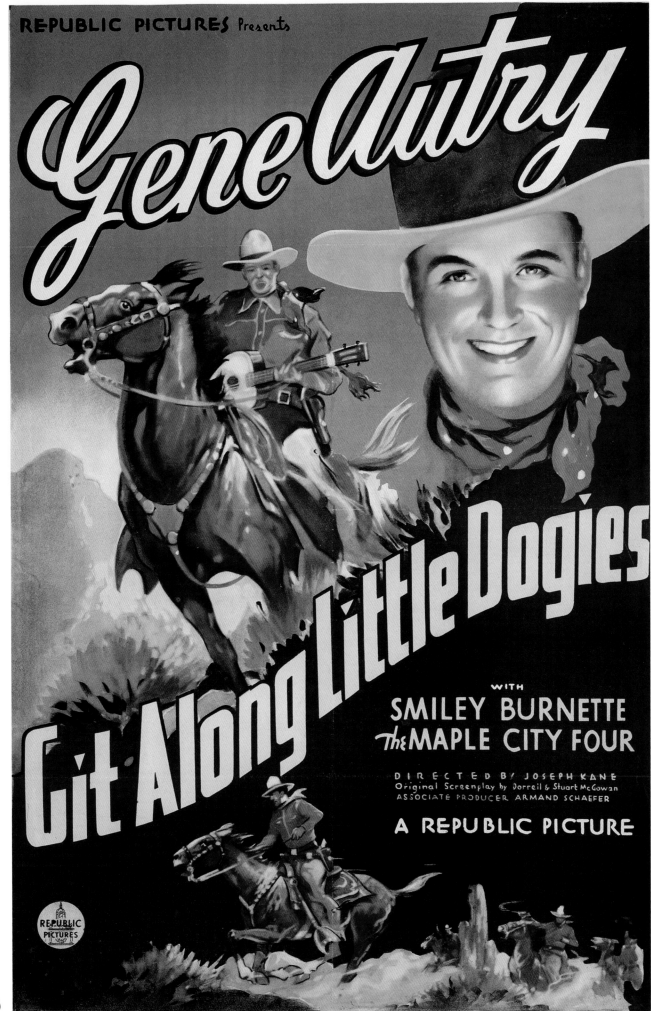

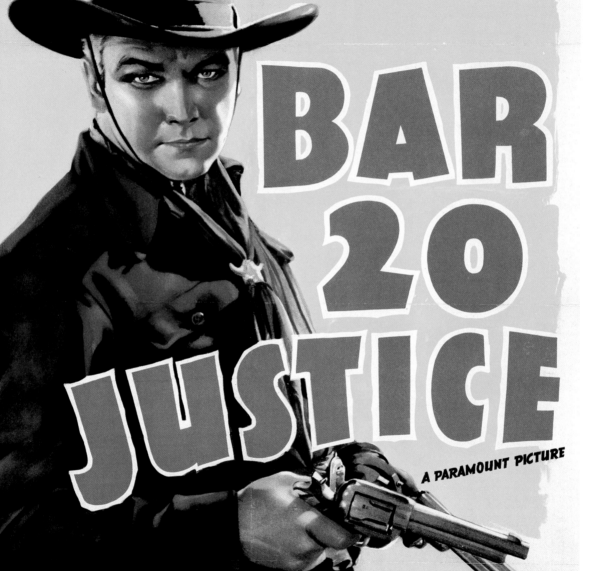

ADOLPH ZUKOR PRESENTS

CLARENCE E. MULFORD'S

BAR 20 JUSTICE

A PARAMOUNT PICTURE

featuring

WILLIAM BOYD

WITH

RUSSELL HAYDEN · GEORGE HAYES · PAUL SUTTON · GWEN GAZE · PAT O'BRIEN · JOHN BEACH
Directed by LESLEY SELANDER · A **HARRY SHERMAN** Production · Screen Play by Arnold Belgard

40

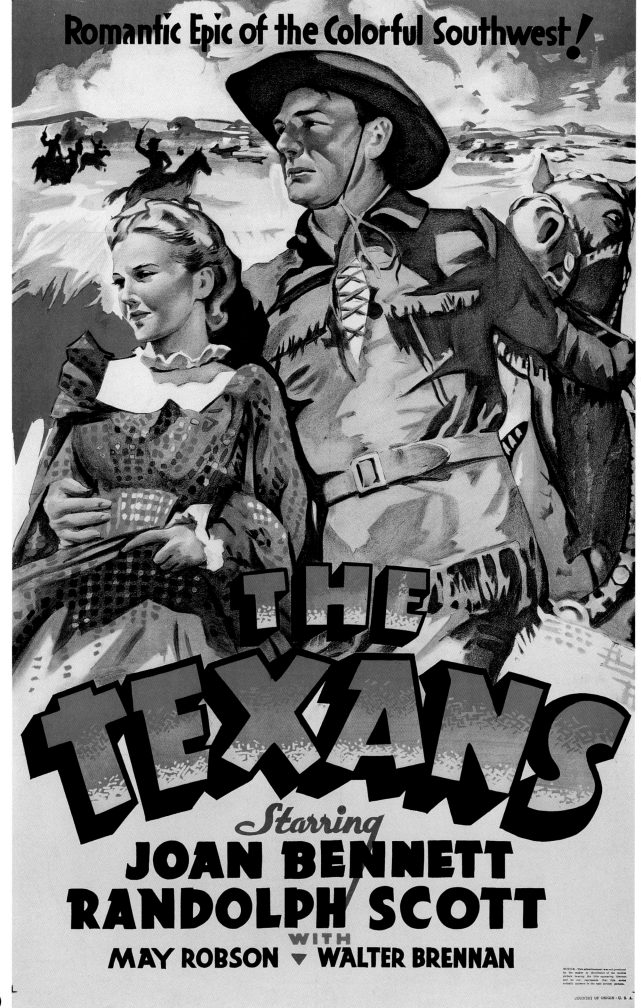

ERROL FLYNN

DODGE CITY

in TECHNICOLOR

OLIVIA de HAVILLAND · ANN SHERIDAN

ALAN HALE · FRANK McHUGH · BRUCE CABOT   JOHN LITEL · HENRY TRAVERS
VICTOR JORY · WILLIAM LUNDIGAN

Directed by MICHAEL CURTIZ ·   ORIGINAL SCREEN PLAY BY ROBERT BUCKNER
MUSIC BY MAX STEINER

A WARNER BROS. PICTURE

44

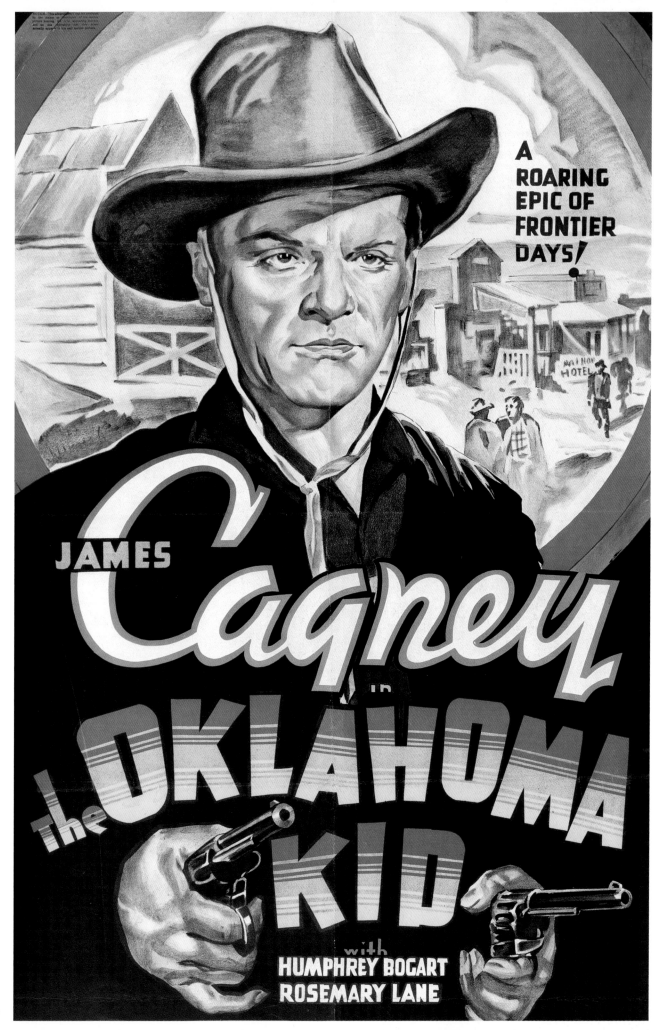

HOWARD HUGHES

presents

The Outlaw

THE STORY OF BILLY THE KID

JAMES STEWART
IN
BROKEN ARROW

COLOR BY *Technicolor*

WITH Jeff CHANDLER Debra PAGET   AND BASIL RUYSDAEL · WILL GEER
ARTHUR HUNNICUTT
Screen Play by MICHAEL BLANKFORT   DIRECTED BY DELMER DAVES   PRODUCED BY JULIAN BLAUSTEIN
Based on the Novel "Blood Brother" by Elliott Arnold

20th
CENTURY-FOX

THE ALAMO

The screen's 12 million dollar spectacle!
thousands in the cast! years in the making!

THE MISSION THAT BECAME A FORTRESS...THE FORTRESS THAT BECAME A SHRINE...

STARRING

JOHN WAYNE / RICHARD WIDMARK / LAURENCE HARVEY

CO-STARRING

FRANKIE AVALON PATRICK WAYNE / LINDA CRISTAL
JOAN O'BRIEN / CHILL WILLS / JOSEPH CALLEIA

AND GUEST STAR

RICHARD BOONE

produced and directed by JOHN WAYNE / original screenplay by JAMES EDWARD GRANT
music composed and conducted by DIMITRI TIOMKIN / TECHNICOLOR®
A BATJAC PRODUCTION RELEASED THROUGH UNITED ARTISTS

They'd never forget the day he drifted into town.

CLINT EASTWOOD

HIGH PLAINS DRIFTER

CO-STARRING
VERNA BLOOM · MARIANA HILL

MUSIC BY   WRITTEN BY   DIRECTED BY
DEE BARTON · ERNEST TIDYMAN · CLINT EASTWOOD

PRODUCED BY   EXECUTIVE PRODUCER
ROBERT DALEY · JENNINGS LANG

A UNIVERSAL/MALPASO COMPANY PRODUCTION
TECHNICOLOR® · PANAVISION®

R RESTRICTED Under 17 requires accompanying Parent or Adult Guardian

CLINT EASTWOOD

THE OUTLAW JOSEY WALES

...an army of one.

CLINT EASTWOOD "THE OUTLAW JOSEY WALES" A MALPASO COMPANY FILM · CHIEF DAN GEORGE · SONDRA LOCKE · BILL McKINNEY
and JOHN VERNON as Fletcher · Screenplay by PHIL KAUFMAN and SONIA CHERNUS · Produced by ROBERT DALEY · Directed by CLINT EASTWOOD
Music by JERRY FIELDING · Panavision® Color by De Luxe® Distributed by Warner Bros. ⑩ A Warner Communications Company [PG] PARENTAL GUIDANCE SUGGESTED SOME MATERIAL MAY NOT BE SUITABLE FOR PRE-TEENAGERS

76/152

CLINT EASTWOOD

THE OUTLAW JOSEY WALES

...an army of one.

CLINT EASTWOOD "THE OUTLAW JOSEY WALES" A MALPASO COMPANY FILM · CHIEF DAN GEORGE · SONDRA LOCKE · BILL McKINNEY and JOHN VERNON as Fletcher · Produced by ROBERT DALEY
Screenplay by PHIL KAUFMAN and SONIA CHERNUS · Directed by CLINT EASTWOOD · Music by JERRY FIELDING · Panavision® Color by De Luxe®
Distributed by Warner Bros. ⓦ A Warner Communications Company

He's got to face a gunfight once more
to live up to his legend once more
TO WIN JUST ONE MORE TIME.

DINO DE LAURENTIIS presents
A FRANKOVICH/SELF Production

JOHN WAYNE
LAUREN BACALL

IN A SIEGEL FILM

"THE SHOOTIST"

Co-Starring RON HOWARD Guest Stars JAMES STEWART RICHARD BOONE JOHN CARRADINE SCATMAN CROTHERS
RICHARD LENZ HARRY MORGAN SHEREE NORTH HUGH O'BRIAN Music by ELMER BERNSTEIN
Screenplay by MILES HOOD SWARTHOUT and SCOTT HALE Based on the novel by GLENDON SWARTHOUT
Produced by M. J. FRANKOVICH and WILLIAM SELF Directed by DON SIEGEL Technicolor® A Paramount Release

UNFORGIVEN

Aug. 7